Media Training

A Guide to Giving Great Interviews

Tim Herrera

MEDIA TRAINING: A GUIDE TO GIVING GREAT INTERVIEWS

© 2014 Tim Herrera, Sacramento, California

All rights reserved. No part of this book may be reproduced or transmitted in any form or by any means without written permission from the author.

TIM HERRERA

MEDIA TRAINING: A GUIDE TO GIVING GREAT INTERVIEWS

Table of Contents

Introduction 9

Media Has Changed 15

Why Give Interviews? 21

Planning ahead for the interview 29

Preparing for an interview 35

You should have questions too 43

The reporter's point of view 51

Can you control the interview? 59

Your key messages 65

Brainstorm before the storm 71

Write down your answers 77

Practice - Out Loud! 83

Interview Ground Rules 89

Interview "Don'ts" 95

Common Interview Mistakes 101

What to say if/when a reporter calls 107

When Media Show Up Unannounced 115

If the media refuses to cooperate 121

Holding News Conferences 127

Communication with Media during a Crisis ……………..133

Important questions for you to ask yourself ……………...141

A dozen steps toward effective communication ………145

Final thoughts …………………………………………...149

About the author …………………………………………...150

Tim's other books …………………………………………153

Thank you! …………………………………………………154

References …………………………………………………155

TIM HERRERA

I'm not an introvert. I'm media shy.
~Steven A. Cohen

MEDIA TRAINING: A GUIDE TO GIVING GREAT INTERVIEWS

Introduction

It's challenging for people to deliver under pressure. When you think of some of the world's top athletes competing and achieving on the highest levels, you know their success is not due solely to luck. They work hard. They train. They train some more. After they train, they analyze their performances to determine what they did well and what needs improvement. Getting good at anything has more to do with practice and hard work than chance.

When you think of some of the greatest musical acts of any generation, you know that while those artists are blessed with certain musical gifts they also have a penchant for training and practice. The only way they're going to get better at something is to train and practice. That's why the best musicians are the ones who work the hardest.

When you think of some of the best interview subjects, you know deep down that they practiced and are prepared to deliver their messages. You watch them on television or listen to them on the radio or on an online feed and you see how they seem to effortlessly handle each question thrown at them. However, effortlessness has nothing to do with it. They work at it. They train for it. Then they get good at it.

MEDIA TRAINING: A GUIDE TO GIVING GREAT INTERVIEWS

Whether it's sports or music or responding to tough questions, getting good at anything has more to do with practice and hard work than coincidence. The same goes for handling media interviews and news conferences. You get better at them through training and practice. I believe that this book will help you with that.

Media Training: A Guide to Giving Great Interviews is an easy to follow handbook that will help you prepare for media interviews and sharpen the skills you need to become successful interview subjects. It's possible if you follow the suggestions outlined in this book, which is written in plain speak with bullet pointed information designed to make the suggestions stand out and simple to follow.

I worked as a journalist for nearly 25 years and saw some very good – and some very bad – interview subjects. The best ones were prepared. They were focused and paid attention to detail. The good ones are respectable representatives of their organizations and of themselves. The not-so-good ones, well… you get the idea.

I feel confident that after reading this book and following the suggestions found within, you will feel confident about giving interviews and standing behind podiums at news conferences. This book is all about preparing you for these types of situations where you interact with journalists and other members of the media.

If you need help developing your public speaking skills and want to become a stronger and more confident public speaker my ebook **Public Speaking: Simple Steps to Improve Your Skills** might be a good start. The tips offered in that book can work hand in hand with the tips in this one.

If you can afford to hire a professional to put you through some rigorous media training to help you become a well-rounded communicator, then you should spend the money and do it. However, that type of training is expensive, yet worth it in the long run.

If you don't have the money to spend on such training, then please read through this book and follow all of the tips within it. It will help you a great deal.

Remember that the best athletes, the best musicians and the best interview subjects work hard at being good. I am happy that you are willing to do the same. Enjoy!

MEDIA TRAINING: A GUIDE TO GIVING GREAT INTERVIEWS

TIM HERRERA

Whoever controls the media, the images, controls the culture.
~Allen Ginsberg

MEDIA TRAINING: A GUIDE TO GIVING GREAT INTERVIEWS

Media Has Changed

The media world is changing so rapidly that it's hard to keep up with everything. The morning drive newscast, the morning newspaper and the evening newscast used to be the prime sources of information. All of that has certainly changed.

Now we get news alerts on our cell phones and through email. If big news breaks somewhere, the information is out there quickly. The immediate information we get isn't always accurate because news organizations are focused intently on being first rather than being accurate first, but still long are the days of waiting to go home to receive the news. Now the news comes to us.

For better or for worse, that's the way things are done now in the fast-paced information gathering and dissemination business and potential interview subjects have to adapt and roll with the punches.

MEDIA TRAINING: A GUIDE TO GIVING GREAT INTERVIEWS

I was a television news reporter way back in the ancient 1980s and that business has evolved at the speed of light. Back then, we shot our stories on video but it wasn't digital. When I say "we," I am referring to a team consisting of a reporter and a photographer. When covering a news story – way back when – we would drive to several locations, interview people, return to the station, view the videotape, write the story, edit the story and run it on an evening newscast. If the story had some immediacy, the station would send out a special truck to meet us and we would feed the story back to the station via microwave where it was recorded on videotape there, then broadcast on television.

It sounds like a media history lesson.

Fast forward to today: A news "crew" might consist of only a reporter with a camera. The term now is Multi Media Journalists (or MMJ). The MMJ does the work of two people in the field gathering information. Sometimes a reporter will work with a photographer as a team. The team will gather their information – interviews and pictures – edit their story on a laptop computer, sometimes in a news vehicle or sometimes at a Starbucks. If an interview subject is too far away and time is precious, the reporter might interview the subject via Skype rather than in person. After the story is edited it is often uploaded to a server. From the server, someone back at the station downloads the story and it's ready for broadcast. The present day process is much faster than ever and it seems to be getting faster all of the time.

Why am I telling you all of this? Because it's important to know that the media works differently these days and that will impact how you respond if and when you are asked to be interviewed for a news story, or if you are giving out information at a news conference.

The news business is lightning fast now. The 24 hour news cycle craves content. Reporters, photographers and other news people are constantly shoveling coal into the news furnace. And it's not just the employees at the news stations who are contributing content. During the Boston Marathon bombing news coverage, we saw hours and hours of video shot by regular people using their smart phones or camcorders.

When dangerous weather wreaks havoc in some part of our country, we see iPhone pictures of funnel clouds and video of hailstorms on TV.

If you see earthquake footage on television, chances are the video was captured by regular folks.

Journalist Paul Bradshaw (2013) says because of today's technology that anyone and everyone can be a news contributor.

> "The blogs of September 11; the camcorder images from the Asian tsunami; the mobile phone images of July 7; the Facebook pages of Virginia Tech. If you needed to read about any of these major events, you could do so – if you wished – without opening a newspaper or watching TV," says Bradshaw.

MEDIA TRAINING: A GUIDE TO GIVING GREAT INTERVIEWS

In addition, online distribution is now a huge part of a journalist's job description. They are not only submitting stories for the newscast – or newspaper or magazine – but they also are providing video and other content for the news organization's website. They are writing blogs. They are posting on Twitter. They are sending information to every possible outlet.

So, if you are a potential interview subject, like a business owner, a government official, or a nonprofit operator, you really need to be prepared and on your toes. There's a chance of you being interviewed or a chance that you will take part in a news conferences to distribute important information. You need to be prepared.

Media has changed. News and information gathering is constant. If you are the person who will be giving the interviews or distributing the information, you have to be ready. There are steps you can take to ensure you are equipped and organized if and when that time times. It's a matter of preparation and practice.

A question you might be asking yourself is "Why would I want to be interviewed by a news person in the first place?" One answer is that you might not have a choice. It might go with the territory of your job. Another answer might be that you know you need to give interviews to promote your company, agency, organization or even yourself. You might not want to give interviews, but you might NEED to give them.

Keep that thought as we move to our next section and get into more about the "why" of interviews.

Societies have always been shaped more by the nature of the media by which men communicate than by the content of the communication.
~Marshall McLuhan

MEDIA TRAINING: A GUIDE TO GIVING GREAT INTERVIEWS

Why Give Interviews?

Many people in leadership and management positions work hard to avoid giving interviews. In fact, if they put as much effort into preparing for interviews as they do avoiding them, they would make excellent interviewees. In many cases, these people might complain and ask point blank "Why give interviews?"

I am glad that hypothetical person asked because here are some reasons.

Interview segments are now a major part of broadcast news programs, especially the cable news outlets. According to a study by the Pew Research Center, airtime devoted to live events and live news reports continues to increase.

The report's authors (Jurkowitz, et al.) state one of the main reasons for the increase in interview segments is cost. According to the report: "This shift means that a good deal of on-scene reporting has been replaced with interviews, which, although they may be live, are far less expensive to produce and do not require a correspondent or crew."

MEDIA TRAINING: A GUIDE TO GIVING GREAT INTERVIEWS

These segments are cheaper to produce and during era of the 24 Hour News Cycle with so much time to fill, networks are scratching for ways to provide content. Filling that content void also includes the Internet as well. The Web and the TV are close to becoming one very soon and both of those segments of the media are voracious and just devour content.

There is no denying that the media landscape is continuously evolving and it is important for people in leadership positions to be able to deftly distribute information to the media.

Many years ago when I was working as a television reporter in Dallas, I was the City Hall reporter covering local government affairs. On one occasion, I was working on a story involving garbage pickup and how citizens were unhappy with how the department was (or wasn't) doing its job. I approached the head of that department, asked specific questions and relayed consumer complaints. I approached without a photographer, so I didn't think this was a threatening situation. However, the sanitation department head – who was a fairly high level person – had no idea how to respond. I knew he wasn't accustomed to being interviewed and it showed and he gave me a stare that said "Why are you asking questions?"

My point here is that people have questions and if you are in the same type of position at the head of the sanitation department, then you need to be prepared to answer questions from the media.

If you are a government official, run a business, or might have any contact at all with the media, here is a list of basic reasons why you should give interviews:

-The public always has questions about your work.

-You want to tell success stories about your agency or organization.

-You are proud of accomplishments and want people to know. If you are a government official then you want people to know government works. If you run a business then you want to promote your company.

-You are representing your agency and likely should be the person to address the media.

-You want the right information to get out there.

-Media coverage can be an opportunity to "sell" your programs and accomplishments.

-Interviews are an opportunity to promote your programs, your people and your achievements.

-Media educates the public and influences public opinion. Consider media coverage an opportunity to educate people about your group or organization and how you can help influence public opinion.

-Press coverage and media attention can be just as effective if not more effective as any other type of advertising and unlike advertising media interviews are free.

If you are a government official of some kind then you know that the public is very curious about what goes on in their government and they should be curious. People want to know where their tax money is going. They want to make sure their government is working for them. And if you are in this type of position, don't you want to properly inform the public? The answer is yes, you do.

MEDIA TRAINING: A GUIDE TO GIVING GREAT INTERVIEWS

The same goes if you run a business or non-profit of some type. People will have questions about what you do and why. Interviews provide a good opportunity to promote what you or your agency do and how well you do it.

Media questions can come during both good and bad times, so it's good that you are preparing for this.

Interviews provide people with the opportunity to share positive news. There's a strong possibility your organization has good news to share. Interviews give you that chance to share. In many cases, the focus of the interview will not be specifically on your "good news" but that does not mean you can't offer information to the reporter/interviewer to offer a wider perspective of what you and your organization do and how you do it.

Interviews present a great opportunity to tell the public about the great things your organization has achieved. Record sales. Increased emergency response time. An increase in the number of people served through a particular program. This is the chance for you to spread good news.

As the person in charge of your organization – or as one of the people in charge – giving interviews to the media is your obligation and an opportunity to represent. The general public likes to hear from leaders. They like to associate the faces with the companies or organizations in their communities. They especially like to know people representing the government agencies serving them.

Of all the points listed above, wanting to get the right information out there might be the most important. It is vital that the public know the right information about what your organization/agency/company is doing and there's no one better to relay the right information than you.

Giving interviews provides you with the opportunity to take control of a situation and make sure the public knows the right information. In so many cases, someone in an opposing position spreads inaccurate stories about a person or group. A good interview can prevent misinterpretation from happening. The public needs to know all sides of a story, any story. Wouldn't you want to be represented fairly if someone were spreading falsehoods about you?

These are just a few reasons to give interviews. There are more reasons and you can develop your own list. Just remember that you should do media interviews because people are curious and by giving interviews you have the opportunity to spread good news about you and your organization.

Remember that giving interviews, interacting with the media, or holding news conferences are things you can and should do, especially if you are in a leadership position. You might get a call from a reporter or a blogger who wants to talk with you. While you are under no real obligation to respond – unless you are a government official – this is something you really should do.

As we know, interviews involve a lot of questions. However, as a potential interview subject, you should have questions of your own before the process starts. That's what we are discussing in our next section.

MEDIA TRAINING: A GUIDE TO GIVING GREAT INTERVIEWS

TIM HERRERA

I'm really grateful I grew up in a house in which media literacy was a survival skill.
Chelsea Clinton

MEDIA TRAINING: A GUIDE TO GIVING GREAT INTERVIEWS

Planning ahead for the interview

In order to be a successful interviewee you have to be a planner. If you have been a fly-by-the-seat-of-your-pants person until now, I hope that you will consider breaking that habit and doing things differently. I hope you will consider becoming a planner, at least when it comes to interviews.

If you know that you are going to be giving an interview, or standing at the podium at a news conference, or making a public announcement to the media, then please know that planning ahead gives you the best chance of succeeding. Not planning at all gives you the best chance of messing things up. You don't want that to happen.

If you and your spouse, or significant other, were going on vacation would you wake up one morning, drive to the airport with no luggage, walk up to a ticket counter and buy a ticket to somewhere, anywhere? That's doubtful. Chances are you would have your details planned out as to where you are going and have everything figured out right down to the penny of what you have to spend. You should approach interview planning with the same attention to detail.

MEDIA TRAINING: A GUIDE TO GIVING GREAT INTERVIEWS

Several years ago, I was working for a State of California agency that oversaw a reward program for unsolved murders. In one particular case, our agency was hosting a news conference with a local law enforcement agency to announce the establishment of a reward for information that would lead to the arrest and conviction of the suspects responsible for an unsolved homicide.

Prior to the news conference, I spent time with the law enforcement agency going over the details of the case as well as details about the reward program, which was fairly successful in helping investigators get information about unsolved cases. I spent time jotting down notes about some specific instances in which this reward program helped close cases.

At one point during the news conference, a reporter asked for specific examples of unsolved murder cases where this reward program had some impact. I was able to share such information because I was prepared. Details are important.

If you have an interview approaching you have to be prepared too. You don't want to embarrass yourself or your organization. If you are in a leadership position, you want to avoid looking like a weak leader.

Communication expert Dennis Bailey believes being truly prepared is the best way to avoid problems during news conferences and interviews. Problems such as unclear information, conflicting facts, and signs of weak leadership.

"All of this can be avoided with a bit of preparation beforehand and by setting a clear goal for what you want to achieve in the interview," says Bailey.

Before your interview, as you are planning ahead, here are some suggestions that will contribute to your successful preparation, which enhances your chances of a successful interview or news conference:

-Do your homework! Learn as much as you can about the situation or issue so that you are as informed as possible. In addition to doing your homework about the issue at hand, also do some homework about the reporter and the media outlet involved in the interview request.

-What do you know about the media outlet interviewing you? Is it a conservative media outlet or does it lean to the left politically?

-What do you know about the reporter who contacted you? Is this reporter a straight shooter or someone who reports stories with a sensational flare? A Google search or a search on that news organization's website should give you enough information.

-While you are making arrangements to meet with the reporter beforehand, you can ask "What areas would you like to cover in this interview?" That will help you prepare. Once you know the general topic then you can begin developing a list of questions you might be asked. Go over those questions and develop your answers.

-Think of questions you would **least** like to be asked and frame answers to those questions. In many cases, a reporter is going to ask some challenging questions and you must be prepared to answer them. Think about the toughest issues you and your organization are facing and develop some solid answers to those questions. While you might not be asked questions you don't want to be asked, at least you are prepared.

This all makes sense if you carefully look at the planning process. Planning ahead for your interview will save you any potential grief after your interview or news conference. Even if you plan for questions that are never asked or plan for scenarios that never materialize, wouldn't you feel better knowing that you had a solid plan just in case?

If you are a planner all of this should be second nature to you. If you are not a planner by nature, start working in that direction because it will help you in the long run. Just remember to do your homework, ask the interviewer questions before you are questioned, and think of questions you'd rather not have to answer. Just follow this basic plan and you will do well.

There is a lot more to the media interview preparation process as you will see when we move along to the next section. Preparation is definitely the key to success. You have to know your information and know it well. You also have to do your share of homework, as you will see when we continue.

TIM HERRERA

We need to police ourselves in the media.
~Bob Woodward

MEDIA TRAINING: A GUIDE TO GIVING GREAT INTERVIEWS

Preparing for an interview

As I mentioned, there's still more work ahead as you fully prepare for your media interview or your news conference. However, it's good and satisfying work that will make you feel more self-confident.

In this section, we are going to talk more about doing your homework. In the previous section, we talked about how you need to spend time researching the reporter or news agency that wants to interview you. Now that you've done some of what we can call "external homework" let's now do some "internal homework." Yes, there are a few different kinds of homework.

If you have already established why the reporter wants to interview you, or you know the general theme of the interview or the news conference at which you are speaking, now it's time to make sure that you have all the information needed to perform well. And you really should consider it a performance because that's what it is.

MEDIA TRAINING: A GUIDE TO GIVING GREAT INTERVIEWS

You have already composed a list of possible questions and developed some solid corresponding answers. At this point, you want to make sure you are not stressing out too much about the questions you'll be asked because there is no way you can think of every possible question. There are too many alternatives.

Brad Phillips, a former CNN reporter and now an author and media trainer always advises people not to over-think when it comes to compiling lists of potential questions.

"Spokespersons don't need to prepare for every possible question. They just need to prepare for every *type* of question," says Phillips (2011).

And what do you think Phillips means by "type of question"? Notice that he is very specific. By "type" he means what subject matter areas will be covered in your news conference or interview. Type can cover a lot of territory: financial, logistical, organizational, or any other specific area that might be connected to your business, product, service or cause.

One area I left out is "hypothetical." Avoid hypothetical questions both in your planning and in your actual interviews. Don't speculate when asked a hypothetical questions. Only respond to what you know as facts and do not engage in imaginary, what-if questions.

The simplest way to avoid these types of questions is to answer with something like: "Well, that's a hypothetical question and I don't think we are going to go there." Then move on. If the questioner presses you, then you can say, "Let's discuss what we know." Eventually, the reporter should get the message that you are not going to deal with theoretical situations.

At one point in my career, I worked as a spokesperson for a statewide agency in California that oversees consumer issues. I was being interviewed by a television reporter who was doing a story about hospitals hiring nurses who were less than qualified and who lost their jobs due to back job performance but who kept turning up at other hospitals, doing sub-par work and getting the hospitals into trouble.

One of the reporter's questions began with "What if hospitals were able to…" At that point, I stopped her and told her that if she was asking a hypothetical question that I couldn't provide an answer. She asked why I couldn't and I responded "What if asks that I speculate and I can't do that. I can't guess. I only know what I know."

"WHAT YOU KNOW" is important in order for you to succeed in an interview or news conference.

Here are some things to keep in mind as you continue planning for your interview:

-Make sure you understand the issues. It will be clear to the interviewer if and when you don't understand. Again, do more homework regarding the types of questions you might be asked.

MEDIA TRAINING: A GUIDE TO GIVING GREAT INTERVIEWS

-Make a list of subject areas you are expected to cover during your interview and come up with some material that you can use to address those areas. While there is no way you can think of every question you might be asked, you should be able to think of every subject area.

-As you are writing your list of potential areas, remember that there is a good chance there are things you do not know. If that's the case, ask someone for help. Find someone who does know the right answers.

-Remember that you will have to avoid responding to hypothetical questions because with those questions you are being asked to talk about things you don't know. You don't want to go there.

-Think some more because thinking is a big, big part of the interview preparation piece.

The points above are pretty logical and take a little effort to implement but they are worth it. If you want to show the interviewer that you are a confident person and "know your stuff" then you really have to know it. You don't want to get into an interview situation where you don't know enough about the content to give an intelligent answer.

Some people may feel they are more relaxed in interview situations when they are engaging in a spontaneous give and take. They feel comfortable in a situation where they know a little bit about the subject but are not completely well-versed. My question to that is: do you really believe that's in your best interest? Going into an interview or press conference without doing your homework is like going to take a really big exam without really studying. The results will not be good.

Preparing for interviews is hard work but you can do it – you need to do it – because it gives you the best chance of doing well and representing yourself and your organization in a positive light.

So far, we've been asking a lot of questions and you have been asked to come up with answers. That will continue in our section, where we will ask even more questions. The internal kind.

MEDIA TRAINING: A GUIDE TO GIVING GREAT INTERVIEWS

TIM HERRERA

It appears that the media filters we carry in our heads are like computers: they've been forced to get faster in order to keep up with the demands our high-speed society puts on them.
Roy H. Williams

MEDIA TRAINING: A GUIDE TO GIVING GREAT INTERVIEWS

You should have questions too

Your preparation continues. In this section, we are going to discuss doing more research before you sit down for your interview or stand behind that podium and start fielding questions. This time we are going to discuss gathering information about the person or media organization that will be interviewing you.

You might ask "Why would I have questions too?" The answer to that question is a simple one but will require some explaining.

Earlier, we discussed how the media is different now compared to many years ago. We now have a lot of specialized media outlets. Some are your traditional "straight down the middle" news organizations that report the facts and don't take sides. Some outlets are very conservative and lean right, politically. Reporters and writers for those types of outlets have specific agendas. The same goes for the other end of the political spectrum. Some news organizations are liberal and you can expect them to take a specific slant during a story.

MEDIA TRAINING: A GUIDE TO GIVING GREAT INTERVIEWS

You also have to take bloggers and free-lance "citizen journalists" into account. These people do their writing and reporting from specific points of view. And you need to know those points of view BEFORE your interview or news conference. Knowing the perspective that a particular news agency will be taking on a news story will help you better prepare.

While I was working as communications director for a government agency, I was contacted by a radio station who asked if we could make our top boss available for a live interview with one of their talk show hosts. These interviews are always a good opportunity to promote the good work being done, and I told the caller I would get back to her as soon as possible. (Please remember that I just said something about collecting your thoughts and getting back to a caller later because we will focus on this aspect more later on.)

In this case, I was not that familiar with the talk show host, so I did some homework. It's a good thing that I did. I went on Google and I went on that station's website and listened to audio clips of the host. I also read the host's blog that appeared on the station's website. It turned out that the talk show host was an extremely conservative type and I suspect right away the way he would ask his questions.

After doing this homework, I conferred with my boss. We agreed the interview was a good opportunity and we formulated our possible responses based on questions that we suspected would come from the host's point of view. It turned out that we were right on and that little bit of research helped a great deal.

Before you do your interview or make your news announcement, you should have some questions too. You need to do more homework, on the news agency, website, blogger or reporter.

Aside from using Google – or the search engine or your choice – there are plenty of resources available to help you answer these types of questions. Jeremy Porter, editor of the blog Journalistics, suggests that potential interview subjects also use databases specifically designed for these types of situations.

"Most media relations databases have pitch tips and other information to help you understand the journalist in advance. Read these, but also assume that the information could be wrong. Do your own homework and READ what they've written to best prepare your spokesperson," says Porter (2013).

After doing your Internet searches, or after mining for information on the previously mentioned databases, you need to ask yourself some serious questions:

- Will the questions from the interviewer be slanted or will they be fair?

- Does the reporter have a specific agenda?

- What is that specific agenda and can I respond to it?

- Will the reporter only look at the issues from his/her point of view?

- Will all of my responses be used or will the positive parts be edited out?

- How will I be able to handle questions from interviewers with specific agendas?

MEDIA TRAINING: A GUIDE TO GIVING GREAT INTERVIEWS

If you have background information on the interviewer, and it appears that this person might be the type of "journalist" who reports from a certain point of view, then you need to ask yourself these types of self-reflecting questions we just discussed.

Keep in mind that the majority of reporters and interviewers are straight-shooters. While they might not be thoroughly informed on the issue at hand, they are not likely to try and portray you in a negative light. However, keep in mind that some interviewers might take an adversarial approach. You have to be prepared for that possibility.

It's not that you should always be suspicious of interviewers, but you should certainly always be cautious. You need to consider what is in your best interest and the best interest of your group, company or organization.

Prior to your interview, there are a lot of questions you can directly ask the interviewer over the phone before you formally meet. Asking these questions will help you get organized and also let the interviewer know that you are prepared:

-What is your story about?

-What particular aspect are you focusing on?

-What is your approach to this story or issue?

-Can I ask how much you know about this issue?

-Can I send some background information?

-When is your deadline and I'll get back to you?

These are not questions that should stay inside your head. Asking the interviewer these questions will help you focus and (hopefully) calm you down as the interview approaches. While you will be on guard, so to speak, you also will be confident and prepared.

Remember that in these types of question and answer exchanges between two people, there are two different points of view. There is your point of view and there is the reporter's point of view.

That is what we will discuss in the next section. Please read on.

MEDIA TRAINING: A GUIDE TO GIVING GREAT INTERVIEWS

TIM HERRERA

I grew up in a poverty-stricken neighborhood, but I didn't really know I was a deprived, poverty-stricken child until the media made me aware of it.
Ving Rhames

MEDIA TRAINING: A GUIDE TO GIVING GREAT INTERVIEWS

TIM HERRERA

The reporter's point of view

People have different points of view. If I am driving through a neighborhood with a lot of speed bumps, my point of view might be that I am traveling through an annoying section of town where the residents, and especially the city, want to aggravate motorists. If I live in that particular neighborhood, my point of view might be that I am grateful to have speed bumps on my roads because they prevent aggravated drivers from speeding along and endangering neighborhood children.

It all depends on how you look at the situation. Any situation.

While the majority of reporters, writers and interviewers are, for the most part, unbiased, there is no denying they approach their stories and interview subjects from a certain point of view. Their perspective is likely different compared to yours.

MEDIA TRAINING: A GUIDE TO GIVING GREAT INTERVIEWS

Several years ago, when I was working in communications for a California state agency, I received a phone call from a reporter who had some questions about one of our programs. After a few minutes, I concluded the reporter must have received some information from a state lawmaker who considered one of our programs "a waste of taxpayer money." In fact, those were the words the reporter used. He said he was doing a story on government agencies wasting the public's money.

After listening to the reporter for a while I said calmly, "Well, it seems you've already formed an opinion and have a direction of how to do your story. Why are you calling us then?"

My response made him pause. Then I used his silence as an opportunity to list all the benefits of the program he questioned. Fast forward to the end: He did the story but it was more about people complaining about programs that actually work and help people. The reporter's perspective changed and the story ended up being more balanced that it was going to be originally.

Public relations specialist and writer Ben Silverman reminds us that interviewers and reporters don't necessarily share our perspective. They have their own perspective. So it's up to the potential interview subjects to be able to explain their point of view while understanding where the reporter/interviewer is coming from.

"Remember that a journalist's job is to serve the reader, not a public relations department. Before the interview, tell yourself that you've already got the publicity and now it's up to you decide whether or not you come off as brilliant and helpful or as a big windbag full of hype," says Silverman (n.d.).

What exactly is a reporter looking for when working on a story? What is on the interviewer's mind? What are journalists thinking as they stand shoulder to shoulder asking questions at news conferences?

Here are some reasons – from a reporter's point of view - why they want and need interviews and why they might be contacting you:

-Reporters need information that comes directly from a source connected with a specific issue on which they are gathering information. That's why they are contacting you. Take solace in knowing they want to get the right information from the right person.

- Interviews help explain, inform, and illuminate. Without interviews writers and reporters don't have the information they need to write stories.

-Interviews put a "human face" on news stories. The people at home watching, viewing stories on the Internet, or reading a paper or blog won't care much about stories that don't involve people who are being impacted by something.

-Interviews give depth, background, perspective, and personality to news.

-Reporters expect enough background to understand the stories they cover. They often only want to speak with subjects for background information. In these cases, the people they are calling are more of a resource. So they have to field questions in order to provide information.

MEDIA TRAINING: A GUIDE TO GIVING GREAT INTERVIEWS

-If you are in some type of government position, remember that the public has a "right to know". So, unless you are working on some top-secret government program the public has the right to know what you are doing. And you need to tell them.

-The public wants to know. People are curious about programs and services that your organization, company or agency provides.

While you are not sure what is on a reporter's or producer's mind when they are requesting an interview, the list above explains some of the reasons why they are reaching out. It is by no means a definitive list. It's difficult to read minds but the list above explains some of the rationale as to why reporters want interviews.

Keep in mind that your perspective and the perspective of the interviewer are likely going to be different. For example, what you see as a wonderful program that provides help to the needy might look to the interviewer like a useless program that costs money to run, has high overhead and is not helping as many people as the program managers say.

You need to approach every interview knowing that the interviewer, whether it's one person, or a host of reporters at a news conference, might not see things the same as you do and they will frame their questions from a different perspective. Understand that and it will help you have a better understanding of why you are being asked those questions.

Stephen R. Covey, the celebrated author of *The Seven Habits of Highly Successful People*, speaks to this perspective in his book. Habit number five is seek first to understand, then to be understood. That's a great rule to follow whether you are dealing with a crowd of reporters or your spouse. Try to look at the world through a lens other than your own.

In our next section, we will focus on controlling the interview. If you are asking "How can I control the interview?" please realize that the answer is "you can't." But we will discuss what you can control.

MEDIA TRAINING: A GUIDE TO GIVING GREAT INTERVIEWS

TIM HERRERA

Maybe it is the media that has us divided.
~Laura Bush

MEDIA TRAINING: A GUIDE TO GIVING GREAT INTERVIEWS

Can you control the interview?

If you are someone that others, even those close to you and who love you dearly, consider a control freak you might have some challenges reading this next section. We all would like to have control over all aspects of our lives but in reality that's not possible. Some things are within your control. Many things are not. When it comes to giving interviews or hosting news conferences, a lot is not within your control.

Several years ago, I worked for the communications department for a California state agency that was planning to sell unused inventory that filled a massive warehouse. The inventory involved items ranging from old computers, to office equipment, to art work. You name it, we had it in storage. It was going to be like a gigantic garage sale.

We fielded media requests from around the world. Outside the warehouse, on the day of the sale, hundreds of people lined up in pursuit of bargains. Inside the warehouse, reporters and photographers lined up to document the frenzy. Once the doors opened, the situation was difficult to control. It was also difficult, if not impossible, to control the interviews.

MEDIA TRAINING: A GUIDE TO GIVING GREAT INTERVIEWS

Reporters broadcasting live from inside the warehouse asked me for interviews. Some of the reporters were the "straight shooter" type. Others were "off-the-wall and goofy" type. With the off-the-wall type, you were never sure what kinds of questions they would ask. During the event, one of those types of reporters asked to interview me and during the interview he asked some fairly silly questions. They were more for humor than information but in the end, the overall interview was fine.

I knew there was no way I could try and control that interview and I had to deal with that truth. In a situation like that, I knew I could not control the story or its outcome, I could only control myself and what I said. T.J. Walker, the founder of Media Training Worldwide, says that is really the only way to approach those types of interview situations.

"You have 100% control over what comes out of your mouth. And, ultimately, that gives you substantial influence over the story's content and the outcome of the interview," says Walker (n.d.).

With regards to control, keep the following matters in mind as you approach an interview or news conference situation:

> -Is it possible to control the interviewer? The short answer is no. You really can't control the interviewer. You can have certain expectations of subject areas that will be covered but other than that your control is limited.

-Do you have control over the questions you are asked? No. That will never happen.

-It is possible to control yourself? Absolutely. You have total control. At least, I hope that is true. You do have control over what you say and how you say it. You have control over how you respond and react to questions. If you maintain that control, you will succeed during interviews and news conferences.

-You have some control over the environment. If you are hosting a news conference, you can pick the time and place. If you are meeting a reporter in your office, you can control that environment.

-Do you have control over the outcome of the story? Another short answer: no. You have no control over the outcome of a story. Have no expectations that the reporter/writer will produce a story that is 100% to your liking. It doesn't work that way.

-Do you have control over what you contribute to the story? The answer to that is a 100% yes! You have complete control over what you say and do when speaking with a journalist or writer. You just have to remember to exercise good control.

That list makes sense because deep down you know you really cannot control others, unless they happen to work for you. When working with the media there are certain expectations you should have about being treated civilly and politely, but have NO expectations that you will be able to completely control the interview situation. Once you make peace with that you will be able to enter these situations with a greater sense of calm.

MEDIA TRAINING: A GUIDE TO GIVING GREAT INTERVIEWS

You cannot control others. You can control yourself. That's certainly the case whether you are in an interview situation or in real life.

We've spent a lot of time on how you are going to approach the interview and how you need to prepare. One of the biggest parts of any interview is the message itself and that is what we will look at in our next section.

Media play a powerful role in establishing and perpetuating social norms.
~Jackson Katz

MEDIA TRAINING: A GUIDE TO GIVING GREAT INTERVIEWS

Your key messages

Now we are going to discuss what you are going to say and how you are going to say it. It has taken a while to reach this point but it was important that we went over all of the other information first.

It's important that you spend time figuring out your key messages, those three to five sentences or phrases that you really want to drive home. With your interview or news conference approaching, you can't just wing it. You need prepared messages. You need the types of messages that make your point and express your position, or your organization's position on an issue.

Key messages are also often called talking points or message points. You will use them to communicate with your target audience during interviews or news conferences. Remember that while you are responding to questions from interviewers, you also are reaching out to an audience. These messages are important to have, important to keep, and vitally important to commit to memory.

MEDIA TRAINING: A GUIDE TO GIVING GREAT INTERVIEWS

I hate to say this but put this book down for just a few minutes. Go over to your computer and do a search using the term "key message points." You'll find thousands of results from just about any organization that you can think of: universities, businesses, sports teams, associations, politicians. Key messages are an integral part of your communication effort.

The key to developing and using message points is to make sure that what you are saying is clear and understandable. You don't want anything that you say to create mixed messages, or sound as if they have double meaning. In most cases, straight talk should produce straight results.

Media expert Kristen Saulnier advises people to spend quality time crafting their messages before delivering them. She writes (n.d.): "Effective messaging involves careful consideration of your campaign's purpose, goals and audience – factors that you've already researched through your media advocacy preparation."

Preparation is vital. There are a lot of things to consider when preparing your key messages. First, you have to consider what the important points are that you need to make. What is the subject area? If someone will be asking you about a program your agency operates figure out the main points of that program that you want to highlight.

If you are preparing for a news conference designed to focus on your new company, narrow down a short list of salient points that you want to share. Basically, your messages depend on the subject and that is pretty simple. And in this case, in any case, think in terms of using bullet points instead of paragraphs. Bullet points are easier to read and follow rather than trying to keep your place while reading paragraphs.

Here are some things to take into account when developing messages and message points:

-Be concise and to the point. Long responses are not good responses.

-Try to keep your list of messages to between three and five key points. If you go beyond five points, you risk losing your listener who is trying to focus on what you are saying.

-Try to accentuate the positive and de-emphasize the negative. You want to remain upbeat if you can, depending on the topic of the interview.

-Make your messages consistent. They need to fit together like puzzle pieces. Conflicting messages send mixed messages.

-Stay focused on the interviewer as much as possible. Glance at your notes to help stay on-topic, but try to maintain eye contact with those doing the questioning.

-Be deliberate with your messages. They all must have a point.

-Make your messages simple and easy to remember.

-Use simple words and language when possible. Sometimes, we do have to use specific words and terminology, but speak as plainly as possible.

-Be honest, believable and credible.

Sometimes speakers are able to memorize key messages they are using, but you must make sure that what you are saying does not sound too rehearsed. You don't want to seem robotic.

In many cases, it works just as well to concentrate on using key words and phrases that can help you make your point.

A lot goes into message development. You will find plenty of books and helpful articles on this subject. Refer to them if you feel the need, but what key message development really boils down to is this: What are the main things you want the interviewer(s) to come away with after you are done speaking and/or answering questions? What do you want people to remember most?

Figure that out and you've nailed it. Of course, you should not be alone in the message development process, or the interview preparation process. You need other points of view from members of your own team.

In our section, we will discuss how you need to reach out for help because no one has the corner on good ideas.

TIM HERRERA

What the mass media offers is not popular art, but entertainment which is intended to be consumed like food, forgotten, and replaced by a new dish.
~W. H. Auden

MEDIA TRAINING: A GUIDE TO GIVING GREAT INTERVIEWS

Brainstorm before the storm

As you are preparing your key messages, keep in mind that a good approach is to start with a lot of them and whittle that list down to a few solid ones, preferably three to five. Keep in mind that while you might be a fairly smart person, chances are that you need help in determining what messages you want to relate.

No one has all of the good ideas. You probably have some good ideas about the messages you want to use in your interview, but there is a good chance that other people within your organization could have some better ideas. You have to be willing to accept that. You don't want to miss out on the opportunity to consider other good ideas. That is not in your best interest.

The best way to develop good and solid messages is through brainstorming. It is important to approach message development as a team exercise.

MEDIA TRAINING: A GUIDE TO GIVING GREAT INTERVIEWS

Several years ago, the agency I currently work for was looking for ways to get more interest in a program we operate that provides high school diplomas for veterans, and Japanese-American former internees, whose high school educations were interrupted by wartime circumstances. We contacted some of the local media outlets and asked if there was interest in helping us get the word out to veterans. Fortunately, several radio and television stations expressed interest.

After getting confirmation of the interest, our communications team gathered and starting brainstorming ideas of what important messages we wanted to share about the program. Initially, we came up with a fairly extensive message list but knew we had to shave that list down. We ended up with a five message list that served me well during a series of radio and TV interviews. The result was that we got an increased number of veterans applying for long overdue high school diplomas. We credited our list of solid messages with contributing to our success.

We developed that list through brainstorming. The process worked for us and management experts like Scott Berkun believe brainstorming is an effective process.

"By distributing a problem across 5 or 10 people, in theory, you should be able to obtain a wider array of different ideas much faster than any one person could on their own," says Berkun (2004).

You might be a brainstorming veteran, depending on your line of work. However, if you are not, here are some helpful brainstorming tips:

-Get a group together comprised of people whose ideas you trust.

-Clearly define the issue and lay out the topic to your group.

-Set a time limit because brainstorming can go on for a long time if you let it.

-Put someone in the group in charge of writing down ideas.

-Gather as many ideas as possible.

-Consider all ideas. Even consider the silly ones because they might make you laugh and that will relax you.

-Try not to evaluate all of the ideas as you go along. Save the evaluation for the end.

-Evaluate. Select the best three to five ideas.

-Take those ideas and turn them into brief sentences that carry your message.

Brainstorming is a great team approach to problem solving and it is a great team approach to message building too.

This is one situation where you do not want to go it alone. Participating in an interview or news conference is a big deal. You don't want to risk the chance that you might forget some important information in your interview. Working with a team and brainstorming for a series of good messages will help improve your chances of getting the best information together.

If you are not really part of a team and work in a smaller environment, consider contacting a group of friends and asking for their help. You probably have a handful of people that you turn to from time to time for advice. Chances are they would be more than willing to assist you as long as they are well-versed on the topic. That's what friends are for anyway.

MEDIA TRAINING: A GUIDE TO GIVING GREAT INTERVIEWS

When you get that team together, starting kicking ideas around. Make sure those ideas are on-topic. Write down all of the ideas. Evaluate what's been said and trim that list down to the best three to five that help spread the message you want to spread.

As you have likely surmised, writing is a big part of this process. While you will be involved in speaking with interviewers, what you will be speaking about needs to be in written form before it is in spoken form. That is what we will discuss in our next section.

Get ready for some writing.

TIM HERRERA

We in the media are just people with all of people's faults.
~Ben Stein

MEDIA TRAINING: A GUIDE TO GIVING GREAT INTERVIEWS

Write down your answers

Not many people have perfect recall of extremely important facts and figures. Congratulations if you are one of those people because you have a rare skill. If you are not one of those fortunate people with impeccable recall, write your key messages and keep them handy during your news conferences or interviews.

Have you ever watched someone answering questions or giving comments behind a podium? You can tell who is prepared and who is not. The prepared people have their information written and organized. You can tell when they are responding. During news conferences, during interviews too, it is permissible for the interview subject to refer to notes and look up and down occasionally.

There are occasions when an interview subject is responding spontaneously to a question and that is fine as well. Spontaneity looks real. Reading responses word for word looks awkward. Yet a person can still handle themselves professionally behind a podium with a tidy list of written notes.

MEDIA TRAINING: A GUIDE TO GIVING GREAT INTERVIEWS

Write your messages down and have them with you before, during and after your interview. Consider your notes an invaluable communication tool.

Remember, as I mentioned before, speaking off-the-cuff is not a good idea unless you are a great, great interview subject. And there are times when a question you have been asked will not have a corresponding answer in your notes. However, writing down your ideas is the best approach for the following reasons:

-Writing things down helps promote recall.

-Having your answers written down will help ensure your accuracy.

-If you are using numbers and statistics, you need to have them written down so that you remember them correctly.

-Using notes helps you create a guide for others so you can have continuity and consistency in your messages.

Make sure your notes and messages are written down on paper. We are in the electronic age where many people write things down on their cellphones or tablets but this is not a good idea. It's also easier to find your place on a piece of paper than it is on a cellphone or table. Paper is dependable. Also, technology fails sometimes. What if your battery runs out in the middle of your talk?

Here is a little exercise I would like to you try right now. Take a little break from reading. Let's say that you have just been contacted by a reporter who wants to interview you about your company or organization. Let's say they are doing a profile on local businesses or organizations and how they are important to the community.

Take a few minutes to jot down a list of reasons why your agency or group is important to your local community. When you've trimmed your list down to five, read it as if someone has just asked you some questions.

How did you do?

Now, put that list away and try to respond again without using notes. Did you feel you did as well without the notes as with them? Probably not. That is why writing your messages down is important. Refer to them when needed.

I try to make it standard practice to write out – or type out – the messages I want to convey during a media interview. The messages that I use are not comprised of long sentences. They are brief sentences and phrases that I can use. I can glance down at them quickly, remember them, and then form my thoughts. I really suggest that you try this. You will see that it works; however, it does take practice.

Coincidentally, practice is topic that we are going to address in our next section. Many people believe that practice makes perfect. I am not sure if practicing your message points prior to a media interview will make you perfect, but it should help make you more polished.

We have more about that coming up.

MEDIA TRAINING: A GUIDE TO GIVING GREAT INTERVIEWS

TIM HERRERA

New forms of media - first movies, then television, talk radio and now the Internet - tend to challenge traditional codes of conduct. They flout convention, shake up the status quo and sometimes provoke outrage.
~Willow Bay

MEDIA TRAINING: A GUIDE TO GIVING GREAT INTERVIEWS

Practice - Out Loud!

When you were younger and wanted to get better at baseball, you practiced. If you sang in the choir and wanted to audition for a solo for the spring concert, you practiced. And now if you want to get really good at handling media interviews and news conferences, you have to practice.

No one is really good at anything the first few times. Maybe I should say few people are good at anything the first few times, just in case you are a savant in many areas. However, the majority of people need to practice things over and over until they reach a level of satisfactory proficiency.

When I started out as a radio anchor and reporter, I wasn't all that good. I was very nervous in the beginning and made mistakes. My voice needed work. My interviewing skills were nominal. My writing needed a lot of work. However, with a lot of time and effort and many hours behind a microphone, I got better and started moving up to bigger and better jobs. Eventually, I worked as a television reporter and anchor and was fortunate to work and live in some very nice cities: Sacramento, Pittsburgh and Dallas.

MEDIA TRAINING: A GUIDE TO GIVING GREAT INTERVIEWS

Becoming skilled and capable at anything takes time, effort and practice. Since you bought this book, you clearly want to improve as an interviewee and that will involve training. When I refer to practice, I mean more than going over your responses to potential questions in your head or slightly under your breath. You need to practice your answers and responses OUT LOUD.

Media expert Diana Pisciotta believes in the old adage that practice makes perfect, whether you are a rookie interview subject or a veteran.

"Even the most confident individual may find a broadcast interview to be intimidating. But practice does make perfect. If you plan on going on TV frequently, I would highly recommend that you find a qualified media trainer to conduct mock interviews on camera," says Pisciotta (2010).

I completely agree with her that hiring a media trainer is a great idea. However, that can be expensive. If you have the funds, it is worth considering. Working with a media trainer is also time consuming. However, even if you don't have a lot of time to prepare, and even if you don't have a lot of money for training help, there are many things you can do to help yourself. Reading this book is a one step in the right self-help direction.

Practicing out loud is one of the best things you can do to prepare for a media interview or news conference. It helps to verbally respond, in a normal tone of voice, to help you prepare. Doing so helps you determine if your responses sound right.

With that in mind, here are some tips to follow as you practice out loud for your upcoming media event:

-Have your message points handy and written in bullet point format either on paper or note cards.

-Make sure you are stressing between three and five key messages.

-Have co-workers and staff role-play the press and ask you questions.

-Make eye contact with your mock interviewers.

-Take your practice sessions seriously because they are important.

-Make sure your co-workers and staff members ask questions you would expect as well as some really tough questions.

-Practice your quotes and soundbites, but be careful not to sound "rehearsed."

-Be clear and succinct. Keep your answers brief. Don't ramble.

-Record your performance on video or audio and play it back.

-When you review your performance, ask for **HONEST** critiques.

-Keep practicing until you feel comfortable being interviewed.

If you take a close look at the list above, chances are that you have heard all of these suggestions before. When speaking with the media, as with so many other things in our lives, we need occasional reminders of what we already know. Like sitting up straight or using a napkin during meals.

MEDIA TRAINING: A GUIDE TO GIVING GREAT INTERVIEWS

If I were to pick out a handful of suggestions to highlight, I would choose two: Be clear and succinct. Keep your answers brief. Don't ramble. And when you review your performance, ask for **HONEST** critiques. It will not help you at all if your co-workers tell you that you are doing a great job when the opposite is true.

Think of all those people who audition for American Idol who have been told by their friends that they are awesome singers. Then when they actually audition, you can tell that they are not very good. Don't be a delusional American Idol contestant. Ask your friends to be honest with you.

Honesty is important when approaching media interviews, you must be honest with yourself and with your responses. Your interviewer also should be honest with you and let you know what to expect during your interview session. While it's not always the case, you should ask for and expect some ground rules.

That's what we are discussing in our next session.

TIM HERRERA

I think relationships are broken up because of the media.
~Jay-Z

MEDIA TRAINING: A GUIDE TO GIVING GREAT INTERVIEWS

TIM HERRERA

Interview Ground Rules

Everything should have ground rules, whether it's baseball, card games or even media interviews. Ground rules are important because they define boundaries and tell us what we can expect. Ground rules make us a little more comfortable.

When you are about to do an interview with a journalist, or you are about to stand before a bank of microphones for a news conference, you should expect that there should be some rules that everyone involved are be expected to follow.

When I worked as a journalist, I always tried to respect the ground rules of an interview or a news conference. For example, the police investigator standing at the podium, at the beginning of the news conference, might say "We are unable to give you the names of the suspects because they are juveniles and the law doesn't allow us to release the names."

In cases like that, reporters won't ask for the names. Sometimes that type of information comes from another source but at least it didn't come from the law enforcement official who said he couldn't talk about a certain aspect of a case, and we didn't ask.

MEDIA TRAINING: A GUIDE TO GIVING GREAT INTERVIEWS

Regular sit-down interviews for radio and television usually have some sort of ground rules, or at least they should. An interview subject might tell the interviewer, "I cannot talk about the details of the lawsuit." If that's the case, the interviewer should be honest and say "I have to ask about the lawsuit. If you want to respond that you can't talk about it, that's okay."

Not much territory is off-limits during interviews and some media analysts believe that ground rules are an unrealistic expectation.

"Ground rules have gone the way of VCR tapes, yet that doesn't change the reasons why you need to be more vigilant than ever about what you say in interviews," says Joyce Newman (2011), founder of The Newman Group.

It is hard to disagree with Ms. Newman, especially when you see all of the shout-fest interview segments on television, especially on the cable channels. Confrontation does build audiences and that's why so many of these talking-head information shows are packed with confrontation and commotion. However, on the local media market level - where you most likely are involved - chances are that your interview experiences will be civil.

Why is it a good idea to establish some interview ground rules? The reason is because it is important to set boundaries. The interviewer needs to be clear on the fact that there are certain areas you cannot discuss. That interviewer might not necessarily respect the ground rules but you should set them regardless.

Here are some ground rule tips for you to consider whether you are in a one-on-one interview with a reporter in your office, live on the television set, or at a news conference:

-Establish areas that are *not* open for discussion. If the interviewer asks anyway, you can politely and verbally step to the side and offer a reminder that there are some areas you are not at liberty to address.

-Establish the interview length, location, day/time. If you tell a reporter that you have only an hour to spare for an interview, you should expect that the reporter will respect the time limit.

-You have the right to know who is interviewing you. If a newspaper or broadcast outlet confirms they are sending a journalist out to meet you, ask for the name of that person. It will give you time to do some research to learn what you might expect.

-You have the right to be treated courteously, even with tough questions. No one should be treated rudely.

-You have the right to end the interview after a "reasonable" time following the answers to important, main questions. Again, there are time limits set.

-You should know the general content and thrust of the interview so you can prepare. Remember earlier in the book we talked about asking what areas will be covered during your interview. You have the right to prepare.

-You should have a representative with you so that a co-worker or fellow staff member can confirm what you did and did not say. Plus, having someone there that you know should make you feel more comfortable.

MEDIA TRAINING: A GUIDE TO GIVING GREAT INTERVIEWS

All of these tips are sensible and realistic. If a media representative has asked to interview you, then you have the right to certain expectations. You have the right to not comment on certain areas, especially if they involve legal issues. If you don't want to discuss something just because it is sensitive and uncomfortable, that is not a good enough reason. There are times when you must respond to tough questions. Remember earlier in the book that we talked about planning to be asked questions that you really don't want to answer.

However, you do have the right to be treated with respect. As my mother used to say, good manners never go out of style.

In our next section, we will cover a lot of ground that might appear to be negative because we are going to focus on the word "don't." But don't worry because I am positive you will get a lot out of our next section.

TIM HERRERA

We live in a media world simultaneously obsessed with technology and personality.
~Eric Alterman

MEDIA TRAINING: A GUIDE TO GIVING GREAT INTERVIEWS

Interview "Don'ts"

Books like these typically have a section dedicated to "Interview Dos and Don'ts." However, I think that every section of this book contains a lot of dos. So, this one section is dedicated entirely to don'ts.

The goal here is to not sound negative. I just want to provide you with a solid list of things that you should avoid doing during your media interviews. It's a lot to remember and it will take a while for a lot of the suggestions you are about to read to become second nature for you. Give it time.

I spent many years in journalism and asked a lot of people a lot of questions. It's hard being a reporter. It's a challenging, high-pressure job. However, when I left the news business to go "on the other side of the camera" as it's called, I didn't realize how challenging it is to be an effective interview subject. It takes time and practice. Those are both things we have discussed several times throughout this book and will discuss again before we finish. Getting good at anything takes time and practice.

MEDIA TRAINING: A GUIDE TO GIVING GREAT INTERVIEWS

The following is a list of things that you **SHOULD NOT DO** if you want to have success in dealing with media interviews. This list seems long but all of the suggestions listed below are of the basic, common sense variety.

Use this list, together with the rest of the information in this book, to improve your chances of success in dealing with media interviews:

-Don't ask for questions in advance. As we mentioned earlier, you can ask for topic areas for discussion, but not specific questions. Interviewers will not give those to you. Typically, reporters and interviewers will not have a written list of questions any way.

-Don't *s-t-r-e-t-c-h* the truth. If you do, the interviewer will find out and report on the discrepancy. This will make you look bad, and you want to avoid that.

-Don't argue even if you are right. State your case. State the facts. Agree to disagree and then move on to the next question. Don't dwell. You don't want to appear to be argumentative.

-Don't ask to see a story before it is published. That will not happen. Chances are that a reporter or writer will not share that with you, unless the reporter is fact-checking. Fact-checking is a very good practice and you can suggest to the reporter that you are available for fact-checking prior to the story being published or aired.

-Don't allow a reporter to violate ground rules. Be polite and firm. Remember you have a right to be treated civilly and with respect.

-Don't blame anyone for anything. Remain positive throughout your interview but you will not come off well if it appears that you want to place blame.

-Don't ask for/agree to going "off the record." This is a very sticky area. You can offer journalists background information but don't go off the record because the chances are too great that the information will be reported, and then likely connected to you. The only time that it might be safe to go off the record is if you have a good relationship with the interviewer. But even then, I would recommend against it.

-Don't waste the interviewer's time by giving them information about your last fishing trip, son's soccer game or anything that has nothing to do with their story. Small talk if fine before or after an interview, but not during. Stay on topic. Don't waste the interviewer's time or yours.

-Don't ramble while you are being interviewed because the reporter will stop listening to you at some point.

-Don't suddenly assume the reporter is your new best friend and wants to hang out with you or come over for dinner. Keep the relationship professional.

-Don't pester the reporter (specifically the television or radio reporter) about sending you copies of the story because they will likely never call upon you again. You can always find clips on YouTube or on the Internet for your files, or you can set your DVR at home.

There are probably more don'ts that we could add to this list. In fact, just by using some common sense you could come up with more on your own. If you stick to following the list above, and following the list of dos that you find throughout this book then you will handle yourself well.

You can do this. It just takes time, effort and practice. We have mentioned that before, haven't we?

What is important to remember is that as you begin doing media interviews, you are going to make some mistakes along the way. Hopefully, they are not big mistakes. In our next section, we will look at mistakes, the common ones and we will talk about how to avoid them.

There's no denying that television is one of the most powerful propaganda media we've ever invented.
~Jim Fowler

MEDIA TRAINING: A GUIDE TO GIVING GREAT INTERVIEWS

Common Interview Mistakes

As long as there has been media, people have been making mistakes during interviews. I am sure Thomas Jefferson and Abraham Lincoln wanted do-overs in some of the interviews they gave. Interview mistakes are common. That is why this section is called Common Interview Mistakes.

There are some miscues that seem to keep taking place in interviews and it seems that history keeps repeating itself. While there might not be extensive research on this topic, I think any media relations expert you speak with will list a handful of certain errors that keep popping up. Consider them universal mistakes.

Before I get into a list of common interview mistakes, I want to say that I think the most common one is when the interview subject doesn't do his or her homework and tries to appear knowledgeable about a topic when that is clearly not the case. Sometimes that comes from plain old hubris, where the interview subject thinks that they have the situation under control, that they don't need to prepare, and that they don't need to practice. They say, I got this! But in fact, they don't.

MEDIA TRAINING: A GUIDE TO GIVING GREAT INTERVIEWS

Media commentator and presenter Andrew Griffiths believes that when it comes to media interviews people should be prepared and also be who they are. According to Griffith (2014): "If you try to impress the interviewer by being someone you're not, it's uncomfortably obvious. Just take a deep breath, relax, and have an authentic conversation. When you're the real you, you'll make a real connection."

Yes, you will make a real connection if YOU are real. You will make a real connection if you are prepared. And you will make a real connection with the interviewer and the audience is you avoid these common mistakes:

-Being unprepared.

-Getting too nervous and not staying calm.

-Talking too much or too fast.

-Using too much jargon and not using plain and understandable words.

-Faking an answer if you don't know it.

-Not showing confidence and not taking charge of your answers.

-Acting as if the interview is like a normal conversation with a friend. It is not.

-Thinking the reporter is your friend. He/she is not.

-Going off-topic and offering irrelevant information.

-Repeating the same point over and over and too many times during the interview.

We could probably add more common mistakes to the list, but let's avoid the negative and accentuate the positive. When you approach an interview, make sure that you are prepared. Remain calm, slow down a little and don't respond in rapid fire style.

Avoid jargon or other complicated words that are not commonly known. Stay confident, but if you don't know the answer to a question please do not fake it. Tell the interviewer that you will get back to them with the information.

Stay on topic and don't stray. Finally, while you will have a series of messages you want to infuse into your interview, give the same answers but with some variety. You can give the same message without saying the same thing over and over again.

These are all common sense suggestions if you think about it. You also can use these suggestions in other facets of communication and not just in media interviews. If you are having a conversation with a friend or giving a presentation at work, you also can avoid these common mistakes and become a stronger communicator overall.

To this point, we have been helping you prepare for the event involving contact with a reporter or interviewer. You've collected some valuable tools along the way. Now, let's focus on using them more. In our section, we will discuss ways of how to handle yourself when you finally connect with the media.

MEDIA TRAINING: A GUIDE TO GIVING GREAT INTERVIEWS

The media doesn't need a conscience; people need consciences.
~John Hockenberry

MEDIA TRAINING: A GUIDE TO GIVING GREAT INTERVIEWS

What to say if/when a reporter calls

Chances are that you are not going to start each morning saying to yourself "Today is the day that a reporter will call and ask for an interview." You never know if or when you might get a call from a media person. And when you get that call, you need to know how to be prepared to handle the conversation.

One important thing for you to keep in mind if that reporters are regular people. While they don't really have what people would call regular jobs, they are normal people who have spouses, children, mortgages, college loans, family concerns, financial problems and the list goes on. People in media are the type who want to do their jobs, do them well, and finish work on time so that they can go home and coach their kid's soccer game.

MEDIA TRAINING: A GUIDE TO GIVING GREAT INTERVIEWS

Another thing you need to realize is that not every reporter is out to get you. It's true that many journalists look for the big exclusive story that will rock city hall and lead to a slew of indictments, which will lead them to a bigger job in a bigger city. But the vast majority of journalists don't work that way. For the most part, they are regular people with unusual jobs.

With all of that in mind, also know that journalists and interviewers have a job to do and they have deadlines to meet. They work in a deadline-drive profession. The 5:00 p.m. news starts at a specific time. The live interview at 5:05 p.m. starts at 5:05p.m. Reporters have deadlines. Bloggers have deadlines. Everyone working in media has deadlines. When journalists contact you they are attempting to gather information while that dark cloud known as the deadline is hanging over their heads.

If a reporter contacts you seeking an interview please realize that the reporter is hoping you will consent to that interview and meet with them sooner rather than later. That is how their business works.

Knowing all of this, you also should realize that you are not obligated to grant them an interview. If there are too many conflicts in your schedule, you can tell the caller that you are unavailable. If you are too frightened (even after learning all the tools you'll ever need from this book), you can always tell the caller that you are not interested, thank them for thinking of you, and tell them to have a nice day.

If you are a public official, while you are not obligated to grant the caller an interview it is likely in your best interest, or the best interest of your agency if you do so. However, you don't have to talk with an interviewer if you don't want to do so.

As a public agency representative, there is a price to pay if you don't consent to interviews. Have you ever read a line in a news story similar to this? – "Director Jay Walker declined all requests for an interview." And how does that look? It looks as if Mr. Walker has something to hide. Whether he does or not is irrelevant.

But with everything you are learning from the book, you can be fully prepared to handle interviews and should not have to decline any such opportunities.

During all of my years as a reporter, if I had a dollar for every time a person I contacted declined "the opportunity' to do an interview with me I could probably pay off all of my children's student loans. While that might be an exaggeration, it is safe to say that I have been on the receiving end of many interview request rejections.

If and when you do receive a media call, you need to be prepared. When the time comes that you get that call, here are some tips on how to handle the phone call from that reporter seeking information:

-Make sure you get the caller's exact name, title, and media outlet so that you can be completely sure who you are deadline with in this situation.

-Ask about the reporter's deadline. Is it at 3:00 p.m. today or next Tuesday at noon?

MEDIA TRAINING: A GUIDE TO GIVING GREAT INTERVIEWS

-Determine what the reporter wants to know. For this, refer to what we discussed in an earlier section about asking the right questions.

-You don't need to give the caller an interview or response right away. You need time to collect your thoughts and any information you might need for the interview. Get a phone number at which the reporter can be reached.

-Repeat the information back to the reporter to ensure its accuracy. Write it all down.

Just because you are not granting an interview right away does not mean you are evading the caller. You have the right to gather your thoughts. Tell the caller that you or someone will call them back in enough time to meet their deadline. You also can tell them you don't have the precise information they are requesting and that you have to locate the right person who can help you before you can help the reporter.

You also should tell them that your agency or organization has a policy whereby all media interviews must first be cleared by someone in a higher administrative position.

While this last suggestion might not be true, maybe it should be. Every organization should have some kind of policy on how to respond to media inquiries and who should respond. If your organization does not have such a policy, it is best that you develop one. In the long run, you will be glad that you did.

Getting an unexpected call from the media can be overwhelming for people. But if you follow the suggested listed above and follow the suggestions throughout this book, you will be well-equipped to handle them. As I have mentioned several times throughout this book, all of this takes time and practice. Over time, you will develop the skills you need to succeed at giving interviews and hosting news conferences.

Sometimes reporters don't call first to ask for an interview. Sometimes they just show up at your door. That can be very intimidating. In our next section, we will share with you some of the tools you will need to handle those types of surprise situations.

MEDIA TRAINING: A GUIDE TO GIVING GREAT INTERVIEWS

I think the media spends a lot of time fooling itself.
~Penn Jillette

MEDIA TRAINING: A GUIDE TO GIVING GREAT INTERVIEWS

When Media Show Up Unannounced

There are occasions when journalists will knock on your door or walk into your office unannounced and ask for an interview or for some information. It's not always the best way to start your day, but it doesn't have to be the worst way either.

Why would a journalist just show up without calling first? There are many reasons but let's look at a few.

Maybe there has been a series of crimes in your business district. A reporter is doing a story on community reaction. They see your business and walk in hoping to get your response to what's going in in your community.

Perhaps the reporter was assigned to do a story on how local businesses are faring in today's economy. The reporter picks a particular business districts, sees your business, walks in and asks for help with a story.

MEDIA TRAINING: A GUIDE TO GIVING GREAT INTERVIEWS

A more undesirable scenario might be that a story has already broken about some sort of investigation involving a business with which you associate – or even worse it is your business – and the reporter decides to come calling unannounced to catch you off guard. Or perhaps the reporter has been calling and requesting help with a story and you haven't responded because you are not sure what to do.

The possible scenarios are endless. When I worked as a reporter, I was involved in the types listed above, as well as many more. I never liked walking into an office unannounced because it can create a combative relationship but sometimes there is no other way for a reporter to get information needed for a story. And remember, as we mentioned before, reporters have constant deadlines.

Here are some things that you can say or do in the event that a reporter appears at your door without calling first:

-You should always be polite. The reporter might not be working in an adversarial way. Regardless, you can just say something like "Please come to my office and let's talk about what it is you need."

-Take the person to a private office or conference room away from co-workers, employees and other staff. You want to avoid creating a distraction, plus the "alone time" you have with the reporter gives you a chance to think.

-Spend time with your guest asking what he or she needs. Remember in an earlier section that we discussed all of those questions that you have a right to ask. Ask those questions and do so in a friendly and businesslike way. Remember that you do not want to be confrontational.

-Learn the purpose of the visit and the nature of the reporter's story. You have the right to know this.

-Make sure that you ask for a business card or ID with name/title/news outlet. You want to be sure you know who you are dealing with and you want to have a record of the interaction.

-If you are not the person who would decide whether or not to grant the interview or provide the information then you can ask the reporter to wait while you get someone on the phone who would make those types of decisions.

-Remember to be courteous and businesslike. Convey to your guest that you would really like to help but need some time to figure things out.

If you cannot connect with the person who would be giving the interview, it is fine to explain that to the reporter and tell that person you or someone from your organization will be in contact as soon as possible. Then you can call the reporter later and either invite them to return, or graciously decline their offer to participate in their story.

If you do decline, make sure that you have a good and honest reason for saying no. If that reasons is that you just don't want to, you can always tell the reporter that you are just not comfortable giving interviews and say that you hope they understand.

There are times, however, when you might not have a choice over whether you should participate in an interview. If that is the case, you have all of the information in this entire book at your disposal to help you handle the situation well.

Remember that reporters have a job to do and that job involves asking hard questions and meeting unforgivable deadlines. There are times when they might show up without notice and you will have to deal with the situation. If you follow the suggestions listed above, you will handle things like a pro.

At this point, you might be asking, what if I follow all of these suggestions, am polite and courteous and the reporter refuses to leave? Well, that can happen. In our next section, we will offer some effective suggestions to help you deal with that situation.

TIM HERRERA

The media dwells mostly on negativity.
~Bill Parcells

MEDIA TRAINING: A GUIDE TO GIVING GREAT INTERVIEWS

If the media refuses to cooperate

In the previous section, we talked about what to do when a reporter shows up unannounced. Information given in the previous section should help you deal with that. In this section, we will discuss what to do if a reporter shows up – whether scheduled or unscheduled – and refuses to leave or cooperate. It can happen and you need to know what to do in that situation.

You have probably seen the scenario many times on television. An angry person is talking directly into a camera lens telling someone to leave their office or their property. Someone on the other side of the camera is asking questions in rapid fire fashion. The angry person is refusing to answer and keeps asking the other people to leave. In some instances, the angry person puts his/her hand on the lens and pushes the camera.

It all makes for good TV theatre but no matter what the situation, it does not make the person being photographed look very good. You really want to avoid being the person who is being photographed in this type of scenario.

MEDIA TRAINING: A GUIDE TO GIVING GREAT INTERVIEWS

However, this scenario happens fairly often. Let's talk about what to do if you are ever in a situation where an interviewer is refusing to leave after you've asked.

Let's say that you are a private company owner or a non-profit operator and a reporter has come to your location for an interview. At some point in the exchange, the reporter becomes difficult and confrontational and refuses to leave. What do you do? The answer: you politely ask that person to leave. You explain that you have provided that person with what you feel is enough information and you ask that person to leave.

Once you ask that person to leave, they basically have to do as you ask. If not, they can be considered as breaking the law.

According to the Reporters Committee on Freedom of the Press (www.rfcp.org) "Once a journalist or other enters private property to ask questions, he or she gains a complied consent to remain on the property if the property owner agrees to talk. These individuals may become trespassers, however, if they refuse to leave when asked."

If you are ever faced with a situation where a reporter/interviewer will not leave your office after you have asked, please do the following:

- Politely inform the reporter that the interview time is over and that you will not be answering any more questions.

- Politely tell the reporter that it is time for them to leave.

-Politely tell the reporter that if he or she does not leave, that you will be forced to contact security (if you have security guards) or the police.

-If the reporter is accompanied by a photographer, politely ask them to stop photographing.

-Do not harass, threaten or touch a reporter or a photographer's equipment.

-Accompany the reporter as you escort that person from your office or building.

-Document the reporter's actions in writing until the arrival of an administrator.

-Consider discreetly canceling any impending appointments.

-Be business-like and polite the entire time and not confrontational. Remember that you do not want your confrontation playing on the 10:00 p.m. news.

If you are a public official and this type of exchange is taking place in a public place or in a public meeting, then technically you do not have the right to ask a reporter to leave. If the confrontation takes place in an office in a public building, you can inform the reporter that the interview is over and inform them that they must leave.

What the Reporters Committee on Freedom of the Press tells journalists is this: "Always leave when asked to do so."

MEDIA TRAINING: A GUIDE TO GIVING GREAT INTERVIEWS

To summarize, you have the right to be treated politely. If an interviewer is combative and confrontational, you have the right to end the interview and ask the person to leave. If that person refuses to leave, it can be considered an act of trespassing.

Fortunately, these confrontational situations are rare, but they do happen. Hopefully, you will be better prepared now.

We have focused a lot of attention in this book on reporters and interviewers calling you and asking for information. In our section, we will discuss the best approaches for holding news conferences in which you invite the press to visit and question you. Please read on for more tips.

TIM HERRERA

The media works in sound bites. They can make you look like a genius or stupid.
~Kato Kaelin

MEDIA TRAINING: A GUIDE TO GIVING GREAT INTERVIEWS

Holding News Conferences

News conferences are a good vehicle for making major announcements, addressing concerns in your community, or even dispelling misinformation being circulated about your organization or company. When should you hold press conferences? The answer: When you have something fairly important to say or announce.

If you don't have anything significant to offer at your event, you will end of alienating the media. It would be like the boy who cried wolf.

If you have a big event like a grand opening, a major task force meeting, a large grant being awarded from some really rich foundation, let the press know. There's never a guarantee of coverage but there's always the chance.

You can hold a press conference when there's some new research or new developments in an ongoing program to unveil. If you have a new partnership you are proud of, or an innovative product to introduce, it might make for a good story.

MEDIA TRAINING: A GUIDE TO GIVING GREAT INTERVIEWS

One of the first things you have to do is invite media to your event, and give them time to consider covering your event. Typically a week or so is a good amount of time. Any more than that and the media will forget about you. Any less than that and they might not have enough time to plan.

You can invite the media either through direct phone calls to specific media outlets or by distributing a news release that you have sent via email, or maybe even fax. Yes, some organizations still use fax machines, although not many do anymore.

We will not spend time in this book showing you how to craft a news release. That might be another section in another book for another time. For quick help, you can log onto Google – or the search engine of your choice – and conduct a search for "sample news release" or "news release templates" and that should be enough to get you started.

Whatever reason you have to hold a news conference—and it has to be an honest, legitimate reason—here are a few simple things to keep in mind when setting the process in motion:

-Include all the pertinent information in your announcement; who, what, when, where and why? Also include what time your news conference will start.

-Choosing your location is important. You need a place that is easy to find, where there is accessible parking, and where there is plenty of room for media and supporters to attend.

-Be smart about your timing. The best times to host a news conference are between 10:00 a.m. and 3:00 p.m. That window is not too early or too late for media, and your invited quests.

-If you are planning to host your event at your place of business, consider using a large enough room to accommodate a good sized group of people. Place a podium at the front of the room with a few rows of chairs in front. Leave empty space in the back for television news cameras and for people to have a place to stand.

-Have three to five speakers ready. Any more speakers from the podium and you will lose your audience.

-Open with brief statements first and then field questions later. This will give you a chance to state your case before the questions start flying.

-Look for positive angles. Take the high road. Speak about your organization and what you are doing.

-Recognize the pessimists but don't stoop to their level.

-Use a podium and have a logo displayed. This provides instant recognition. It's like "product placement" in the movies.

-Make people accessible after the news conference for individual interviews. During these one-on-one interviews, reporters will ask specific questions not asked during the news conference. However, sometimes they will ask some of the same questions, typically for clarification purposes.

-If your event is away from the office, tell your office staff all the details to accommodate reporters who are running late.

-Prepare handouts for guests, such as factsheets and brochures about your organization. Additional information is valuable.

The most important element: have your information prepared and ready to deliver. Remember all that we have discussed up until this point. Use the tools you have acquired so far. Once you are prepared, you will become confident.

Speaking in public, on any level and in any form, is a challenge for many people. They would rather do anything else than speak before any type of group and make a presentation. That would include participating in news conferences. If you would like some help developing your public speaking skills, my ebook **Public Speaking: Simple Steps to Improve Your Skills** might be a good start. It is the perfect book for anyone who wants to become a strong and confident public speaker and presenter. That book compliments this one nicely.

News conferences take some planning and effort but if you follow the suggestions in this section, you should be very successful at hosting such an event. As you know, news conferences are planned events. But it's the unplanned events that can cause us trouble. As odd as it might sound, you can plan for the unplanned. And that's what we will discuss in our next section.

TIM HERRERA

I'm kind of a gossip hound, but watching the media whip the small fires into giant forest fires so that they can cover the result is infuriating.
~Anne Lamott

MEDIA TRAINING: A GUIDE TO GIVING GREAT INTERVIEWS

Communication with Media during a Crisis

The word "crisis" has many definitions of different lengths and detail. Basically, a crisis is any situation which requires immediate and coordinated action that could have significant impact on the organization or its reputation. A crisis is an unexpected event or series of events that create a lot of uncertainty that can threaten your organization's goals.

During times of crisis, there is a great deal of uncertainty and fear. People turn on their televisions, or log onto the Internet or check their Smartphone, to get the latest information, analysis of the current circumstances, and to make sense of things. Most people look to the media to reduce uncertainty and fear by receiving what they believe to be accurate information.

MEDIA TRAINING: A GUIDE TO GIVING GREAT INTERVIEWS

There are several questions that are raised about this. First, is the information sources are providing journalists accurate? Sometimes CEOs and spokespeople publicly react too quickly, without having all the facts, or the right facts. This can compound the crisis. Also, are the journalists accurately reporting the information? This cannot be guaranteed during crisis situations. It's up to professional communicators to monitor the reporting and speak up when inaccuracies are reported.

The news business today moves at lightning speed. Many stories now are broken on blogs or websites rather than in the Sunday morning newspaper or the 11:00 p.m. news. Newspapers, news radio stations, 24-hour cable news operations and every other media outlet imaginable can have great impact, both negative and positive, on any given situation.

By nature, humans don't really like to plan for crises. Basically, we don't want to plan for the possibility of bad things happening. Every business, every school, and every organization is required to have some kind of emergency evacuation plan in the event of some kind of crisis. For instance, companies practice fire drills. But how many groups or organizations have a media crisis plan and practice it? The answer: very few.

Think of a crisis media plan as being like an insurance plan; you don't really want to use it but when you do you are glad you have it. The best thing to do to prepare for a possible crisis is have a plan prepared and tucked away somewhere knowing that you will only pull it out of the drawer and blow the dust off it in case of emergencies. Think of a crisis media plan like the jack in the trunk of a car; you only pull it out and use it in the event of a flat tire. It's the same with a crisis media plan; you only use it on rare occasions.

Developing a media plan is too complex of a topic to address in this section. Actually, we could devote an entire book to the subject. I suggest that you look for resources that can help you create a fully developed plan.

In the meantime, we can go over some tips:

-Plan in advance for a crisis.

-Create a "crisis management" team that you can call into action quickly.

-Spell out what you want to accomplish.

-Put your spokesperson into action.

-Develop key messages.

-Determine the best channels of communications.

-Stick with what you know.

-Be honest and open with reporters and avoid saying "no comment."

-Relax.

-Consider getting professional communications help if you feel it's necessary.

MEDIA TRAINING: A GUIDE TO GIVING GREAT INTERVIEWS

Hiring an expensive professional communications firm does not necessarily guarantee that you will get better results than if you hired a less expensive company to do the work. But the opposite isn't necessarily true either. However, if you think the job is too big for you then seek professional help.

The following point is worthy of further emphasis. If a reporter is asking about the circumstances surrounding a crisis tell that reporter only what you know. Do not hypothesize. That can lead to more conjecture and more rumors.

Here is another list of things to remember when it comes to crisis communications planning:

-Make it clear that the organization is concerned about the people involved.

-Explain what is being done to remedy the situation.

-Keep the message consistent with all constituencies. Never tell one constituency anything that is not being told to the media.

-Be open, honest, and tell the full story. If you do not, someone else will.

-Never respond with "no comment," instead explain why you cannot answer the question.

-Do not guess or speculate. If you do not know the answer, say so and offer to find the answer.

-Respect reporter deadlines. If you promise to get information, do so as quickly as possible.

-Never speak off the record. The media can use any information released.

This section is worthy of further emphasis. If a reporter is asking about the circumstances surrounding a crisis tell that reporter only what you know. Do not hypothesize. That can lead to more conjecture and more rumors.

Here is another list of things to remember when it comes to crisis communications planning:

-It's better to over-estimate the crisis than to under-estimate it. By over-estimating you will be able to use all the tools that you have in place to solve your problems quickly.

-When you are talking to the media about the crisis at hand remember the order of importance of your concerns: people always come first, property always second, and money is third. You know in your heart that's right any way, but it's important that you remember that sequence, otherwise you could be labeled as cold and callous.

-If the crisis was somehow preventable, prepare a response to the question "how can you prevent this from happening again?" Make sure that your answers are also "solution oriented." Have your solutions ready.

-Monitor the coverage in progress for accuracy. If reporters are making mistakes pull them aside, kindly and politely, and tell them.

When a crisis hits what happens within the first few hours is crucial. Whatever the media reports sets the tone for the event, so the first impression that the media gets from you is extremely important. It's better to be proactive than reactive, so please plan ahead. Someday you will be glad that you did.

MEDIA TRAINING: A GUIDE TO GIVING GREAT INTERVIEWS

True the planning takes place long before there is any crisis. It is really difficult to craft any type of plan if you are creating one on the fly. It's like constructing a house without building plans – you never know what your end product is going to look like.

Now, as you do all of this planning there is one big question in particular that you must ask yourself. We will ask that question in our next section.

Whoever controls the media, controls the mind.
~Jim Morrison

MEDIA TRAINING: A GUIDE TO GIVING GREAT INTERVIEWS

Important questions for you to ask yourself

Are you a Do-It-Yourselfer? Can you watch someone on a Discovery Channel program tear out a wall and put in a home theatre system and think you can do that?

Can you watch a program on the Food Network create a gourmet meal out of kale and tuna and replicate the masterpiece?

If you answered yes to those questions, then you might be the type of person who can handle working with the media after reading and absorbing all of the information in this book.

But if you are not that type of person, don't worry. Even after following the tips in this book, you might not think you are capable of giving successful interviews or hosting successful news conferences. First, I would say that maybe you are and you should give yourself the benefit of the doubt. However, if you come to the conclusion after some deep self-reflection that being "the spokesperson" is not right for you, it is okay because you are not alone.

MEDIA TRAINING: A GUIDE TO GIVING GREAT INTERVIEWS

I give plenty of interviews in my line of work, but I spend more time helping others prepare for interviews and news conferences. I feel it is better that information be delivered by real sources such as presidents, chairpersons, superintendents and executives rather than from trained spokespeople. In my opinion, information coming from real sources makes that information more real.

So, if and when the time comes that you are facing the opportunity to give an interview or participate in a news conference, ask yourself some important questions:

-Am I <u>really</u> the one who should be doing this interview?

-If I am the right person, am I properly prepared?

-What do I have to do to prepare?

-If I am not the right person to speak, then who is the right person?

-Is that person prepared to speak on behalf of us?

-What does that person have to do to prepare?
-Am I/Are we ready to work?

If you have the money, you can hire a professional to do the heavy media lifting for you. But it is expensive. You bought this book because you know deep down that you can do this work yourself, and chances are that you can. However, be introspective. Ask yourself the list of questions you see above and determine how much you can do without professional help.

My guess is that you can do it. It all takes time and practice, as we have mentioned before.

We are coming into the home stretch of this book. The last section is next and in that section we will discuss some very important steps you should follow to improve your communication with others.

These steps will help you whether you are addressing an auditorium during a critical news conference or whether you are talking to a person one-on-one about a personal subject.

Please read on.

MEDIA TRAINING: A GUIDE TO GIVING GREAT INTERVIEWS

Most people treat the news media like the exercise bike they have in their basement. They're glad it's there but they never use it.
~Drew Curtis

MEDIA TRAINING: A GUIDE TO GIVING GREAT INTERVIEWS

A dozen steps toward effective communication

As we wrap things up, I wanted to offer you one final list that you will find helpful in your communication. Whether you are sitting across from a radio talk show host, standing behind a row of microphones at a news conference, or sitting with a reporter for a one-on-one interview, I think you will find value in this list.

Consider following these suggestions:

-Be polite and communicate that you want to help.

-Make sure you understand the issue(s).

-Don't assume that you have all of the answers.

-Get to the point.

-Be an active listener. Listen to their questions rather than think about your next answer.

-Be honest.

-Be prepared but NOT over rehearsed

-Be aware of body language. Yours and theirs.

MEDIA TRAINING: A GUIDE TO GIVING GREAT INTERVIEWS

-Be aware of and accept the fact that someone might challenge what you say. Be prepared for that.

-Be consistent and clear with your messages.

-Know when it is time to step talking.

-Pause and reflect for a few seconds before responding.

It is a logical list that you can apply to many other types of situations, whether it is working with the media or communicating with a co-worker. I hope you are able to use this list to help you improve your communication, at every level.

Final thoughts

These final thoughts will not take long.

Be prepared to live with whatever you tell a reporter or interviewer. There are no give-backs. Once you say something you cannot un-say it.

You have to be really careful with what you say and how you say it. You have to choose your words carefully. You have to speak them carefully.

You have to be confident. In order to be confident, you have to prepare and practice what you want to communicate.

Prepare and practice.

Communicate.

Best of luck!

About the author

Here's some information about me. I am a Communications Director, author, free-lance writer college writing and communications instructor, and a former journalist and radio talk show host.

I worked for 22 years in the journalism business, with most of that time spent honing my public speaking skills in television and radio.

For more than 12 years, I was a reporter and anchor at KCRA-TV in Sacramento where I was fortunate to have earned 14 prestigious journalism awards. I have also worked as a television and radio reporter and anchor in Dallas-Fort Worth and Pittsburgh.

In 2003, I was a runner-up for the Will Rogers Humanitarian Award, presented by the National Society of Newspaper Columnists. I have a B.A. in Journalism from Penn State University and an M.A. in Strategic Communications from National University.

I also have extensive experience in media relations having served as Communications Director for several agencies for the State of California, including the Department of Consumer Affairs and the Department of Conservation.

When I am not working at my communications job or writing books, I teach communication studies courses for colleges that have distance learning programs.

I currently serve as the Communications Director for the Sacramento County Office of Education where I have been fortunate to have earned numerous awards from the California School Public Relations Association (CalSPRA).

For more information visit my Web site: www.timherrera.com.

MEDIA TRAINING: A GUIDE TO GIVING GREAT INTERVIEWS

Tim's other books

Public Speaking: Simple Steps to Improve Your Skills

What the Online Student MUST Know: Vital Lessons BEFORE Logging On

30 Things You Should Know About Media Relations, 2nd Edition

30 Things You Should Know About Media Relations, 1st Edition

Dad, You Are NOT Going Out Wearing That!

From Wedgies to Feeding Frenzies

Where the Dust Never Settles

I'm Their Dad! Not Their Babysitter!

Thank you!

I want to thank you for taking the time to read this book. It means a lot to me. I believe this book will help prepare you for media interviews, news conferences or any other kind of encounter you might have with media.

I plan on updating this book from time to time. If you have some suggestions for me and would like to suggest a topic, please feel free to send me an email at timherrera@rocketmail.com.

I also would appreciate it if you had the time to write a review of this book on Amazon. That will also let me know what additional information readers would like to see in this book.

Best of luck to you!

Tim

References

Bailey, D. (2013, December 3). Five ways media training can help your next interview. . Retrieved July 14, 2014, from http://www.savvy-inc.com/blog/bid/327283/Five-ways-media-training-can-help-your-next-interview

Berkun, S. (2004, July 1). How to run a brainstorming meeting.. . Retrieved July 14, 2014, from http://scottberkun.com/essays/34-how-to-run-a-brainstorming-meeting/

Bradshaw, P. (2008, February 20). Ten changes in 10 years for journalists. Press Gazette.

Griffiths, A. (2014, June 17). Nine common media interview mistakes. . Retrieved July 14, 2014, from http://www.flyingsolo.com.au/marketing/public-relations-pr/nine-common-media-interview-tips

Jurkowitz, M., Santhanam, L., Adams, S., Anderson, M., & Vogt, N. (n.d.). The Changing TV News Landscape. . Retrieved July 14, 2014, from http://stateofthemedia.org/2013/special-reports-landing-page/the-changing-tv-news-landscape/

Newman, J. (2011, September 1). why the Old Ground Rules for Media Interviews Don't Apply Anymore . . Retrieved July 14, 2014, from http://www.presenting-yourself.com/executive-media-training/why-the-old-ground-rules-for-media-interviews-dont-apply-anymore/

Phillips, B. (2011, June 28). Interview prep: 6 types of questions the media always asks. . Retrieved July 14, 2014, from http://www.prdaily.com/Main/Articles/Interview_prep_6_types_of_questions_the_media_alwa_8734.aspx

Pisciotta, D. (2010, May 4). How to Prepare for a Broadcast Interview. . Retrieved July 18, 2014, from http://www.inc.com/guides/2010/05/preparing-for-broadcast-intervews.html

Porter, J. (2013, January 2). How to Prepare for Press Interviews. . Retrieved July 14, 2014, from http://blog.journalistics.com/2013/how-to-prepare-for-press-interviews/

Saulnier, K. (n.d.). Media Advocacy: Developing and Framing Your Message. . Retrieved July 14, 2014, from http://www.tsne.org/media-advocacy-developing-and-framing-your-message

Silverman, B. (n.d.). Public Relations Basics: Preparing for a Media Interview. . Retrieved July 14, 2014, from http://www.ereleases.com/prfuel/public-relations-basics-preparing-for-a-media-interview/

Walker, T. (n.d.). Preparing Executives for Media Interviews. . Retrieved July 14, 2014, from http://www.cyberalert.com/media_interview.html

www.ingramcontent.com/pod-product-compliance
Lightning Source LLC
Chambersburg PA
CBHW072033190526
45165CB00017B/633